THE COMPLI
AIRLINE PIL
INTERVIEW WORK BOOK

MW01485869

Contents

1. INTRODUCTION

Airline pilot interviews have evolved dramatically over the last decade. Gone are the days of two check captains rigorously probing your aerodynamic technical knowledge. Nowadays the interview team will generally consist of at least one member of the human resources department and representatives of flight operations.

The modern airline interview is now centered around the behavioral based concept developed by human resource teams around the world and can seemingly have very little to do with aviation. Behavioral based interviews work on the premise that how you have conducted yourself in the past is indicative of how you will perform in the future.

There are three general categories of behavioral questions:

1. Example Based Questions

2. Negative or Difficult Questions

3. Open Ended Questions

Pilots are very good at what they do but tend to perform poorly when faced with this type of job interview. This work booklet will give you guidance and examples on how to approach and prepare for your interview.

This booklet has been designed to be used in conjunction with the **One on One Interview Coaching as well as our Online Program.** Whilst not designed to provide you with the answers, they must be your own words and experiences, it will help you structure and deliver your responses in a clear and concise manner.

We are here to help, so please do not hesitate to get in contact with us should you feel you have a question that we have not been able to answer for you.

Best of luck!

The Team At Flightdeck Consulting

www.flightdeckconsulting.com

2. THE PHONE INTERVIEW

A ***pre-interview telephone screening assessment*** is becoming an increasingly common tool used by Human Resource Departments around the world.

It is essential to ensure your phone interview is a pre booked appointment and not an impromptu telephone call. If the phone call is taken and you are not ready, explain to the caller that you are not in a position to take the call, take their name and number and call them back at a time that suits you, or book in an appointment that is mutually convenient. This will not be considered rude nor will it jeopardize your chance of success. The phone interview is your first step in getting that dream job it must be treated seriously and not dismissed as just a friendly chat with someone from the recruitment office. Remember to remain professional even if they appear to be overly casual.

 **Tips!**

- Make an appointment for the phone interview and ensure you can take the call at a time that will allow you not to be distracted and you are in a quiet location.
- Remain professional, remembering this is an interview.
- Refer to your notes but don't read from them, use bullet points for reference.
- Stay upbeat, positive and passionate.
- Smile when you talk, this will alter the tone of your voice conveying a friendly, positive demeanor.
- Use short, clear and concise answers.
- Turn Call Waiting OFF!

Whilst the interview will normally last 10- 15 minutes, be prepared to clear an hour of your time so as not to be time pressured. There are several standard questions that must be asked and this will allow you to prepare in advance.

During your preparation write your answers in point form. During the interview this will allow you to refer to your notes whilst still ensuring your answers are fresh, natural and unscripted.

The opening questions will normally confirm the information that they have about you is correct. Your contact information, licenses, ratings and flying hours. Know your CV ***and make sure it is up to date***.

QUESTIONS TO PREPARE FOR IN ADVANCE
- Tell me about your career to date?
- Why do you want to work for us?
- What do you know about our company?
- What do you have to offer us?
- What remuneration are you expecting?
- When are you available to start?
- Do you think you will be able to cope with the flexibility required by last minute roster changes?
- You will be flying with different people everyday, tell me about a time you have flown with someone very different from yourself?

Normally they will then explain the process from here and what to expect, when and how they will contact you should you be successful.

In the chapter on Panel Interviews we have outlined in detail, guidance on answering the above questions. Just remember, have your notes in point form, this enables you to sound natural and unscripted.

3. SKYPE OR VIDEO INTERVIEW

Here are some pointers to help you make the most out of your Video interview.

1. Choose a professional username as with an e-mail address you use. A Skype account with a name like flyboy11 or drunkpants12 is not going to help you.

2. Do a mock run with a friend, make sure your connection will hold a SKYPE call and you know how to use SKYPE before the interview.

3. Arrange the setting you want to be seen against. It should be a clear and blank background with no movement or bright light. You can check out the background by going to: "Tools -> Options -> Video Settings". Make sure that you are clearly visible and comfortably positioned in the "shot" in your chair. If you are using a friends office then take the time to check everything first and make changes where necessary.

4. Turn off your mobile phone, home phone and make sure people know "DO NOT DISTURB". If you're Skyping from home, make your family and pets scarce. Barking dogs or crying children will do you no favours.

5. Try to make eye contact with the camera and not just at your own picture. Gazing at the computer screen instead of the camera while you're talking will put the interviewer off.

6. Dress for the occasion, as if for a panel interview in person.

7. Try to have your point forms near the camera so it doesn't look like you are referring to notes, these can help jog your memory but don't over do it.

Notes

4. THE PANEL INTERVIEW

FIRST IMPRESSIONS

From the moment you walk into the building your interview has begun. Everybody from the doorman to the receptionist is watching you and they will all form an opinion so the old saying about first impressions applies from the moment you walk in the door until you're safely out of the building.

Within seconds of meeting someone a first impression is made and that impression is virtually irreversible. That vital first few minutes of meeting the interviewers, your greeting, handshake, smile and body language will determine how your interviewer will perceive you and the tone for the day will be set. If their opinion of you is positive then throughout the day they will be looking at your actions and answers to confirm their decision, and visa versa if it is negative.

Much of what is required to make a good impression is common sense. But with a little extra thought and preparation, you can hone your intuitive style and make that first impression not just good but great. Just remember you want to be the standout candidate, but for the right reasons!

 **Tips!**

- Dress should be neat, tidy and appropriate. There is no such thing as over dressing in a job interview, however it is best to be conservative.
- A confident handshake, but not too firm, making eye contact with your opposite.
- Have a pleasant and warm smile.
- Make positive small talk, this will help to settle your nerves.
- Be courteous and attentive.
- Have a positive, confident outlook on the day.
- You have worked hard for this day, don't blow it by making a joke that's taken the wrong way. I have seen too many jokes back fire on the candidate, it's not professional and has no place in today's professional job interview.
- Use common sense
- Be yourself, but be the best version of yourself possible. We all like to work with people we like and who like us.
- Turn your phone OFF, don't just leave it on "Silent".
- Watch your small talk, "So your just the recruiter?" Won't go down very well.
- Everyone you meet is part of the interview process. Don't tell jokes to the secretary or ask where the "little boys room" is. Maintain your professionalism throughout.

Notes

_____

_____

_____

_____

_____

_____

_____

_____

THE FORMAT OF A TYPICAL PANEL INTERVIEW

Representatives from both the HR department and Flight Operations will conduct your airline interview.

Questions will be asked in order to cover the following topics;

- About your career
- About yourself
- About the company
- Behavioral questions
- Scenario based questions
- Technical questions
- Your questions to the interview panel

WHAT THE INTERVIEWS ARE LOOKING FOR

There are several criteria the interviewers will test and quiz you on and will need to observe during the actual interview process.

1. Overall personality, will you fit in, are you what we are looking for?

2. How you cope under stress, particularly when you have made an error or mistake.

3. Can you be trained, i.e. are you able to take direction?

4. Your ability to use reasoning and logic

5. Your command potential

1. OVERALL PERSONALITY and DEMEANOUR

Having already done your homework on the style of person your company employs, bring to the table and highlight attributes of your personality that match the company profile

A great resource is to visit the company website and read up on the "About Us" tab.

Your answers, body language and overall demeanour should portray a relaxed professional, someone who is confident in their ability and personality

When all is said and done in reality the recruiters are looking for an individual with whom they will enjoy flying with, is competent and at the end of the day's duty will enjoy a beer with.

2. YOUR ABILITY TO COPE UNDER STRESS

Most airline interviews will lead to a point where the recruiters will test you under pressure, so it is best to be prepared when this inevitably happens.

The interviewer will lead you in a direction of questioning to find a weakness in your knowledge and expose it. How you handle this moment will most likely determine the outcome of your interview.

The Scenario

The interviewers are leaning back in their chairs with a slight grin on their face. You find yourself backed into a corner, unsure of the answer, a little confused and wondering how you might dig yourself out of this hole you've dug for yourself.

Don't Panic! This is a planned and expected part of the interview

Here's how to proceed.

- Structuring your answers as described in chapter 7 will assist you in avoiding this situation.
- Don't be afraid to admit your not entirely sure, be prepared to cut your losses.
- There's nothing wrong with giving your best guess, but be sure to explain your reasoning.
- Stay positive, remain in the interview.

Do Not:

- Make excuses
- Become defensive
- Continue to try and justify your answer
- Act dejected
- Continue to dwell on it to the point where you lose your concentration.

There is a point to all of this, it is essential to demonstrate to the panel how you perform under pressure. In the Human Resources world there is a theory on behavioural patterns. The theory is that how you have behaved in the past is indicative of how you will perform in the future. i.e. when your backed into a corner do you problem solve using logic, experience etc and how well do you recover from errors.

3. ARE YOU TRAINABLE, CAN YOU TAKE DIRECTION

During this stage of the interview the panel will be looking at your ability to be trained and take direction. The questions will generally lead you into an area of technical study you may not be familiar with..

Do:

- Work with them and follow their guidance, take the new information with enthusiasm and a positive approach.

"I hadn't thought of it like that?"

"Of course, that makes sense now!"

Do Not:

- Allow yourself to be put into a position where you might be seen as argumentative
- Become disagreeable or show lack of interest.
- Justify your lack of knowledge in the area.

"I haven't flown the 747 so I really can't answer that question"

4. YOUR ABILITY TO USE REASONING AND LOGIC

The panel will throw a question at you such as

"Describe to us the B747-400 fuel system"

Now, they know you probably have no idea how the 744 fuel system works, they want to see you have a go, use logic and reasoning to provide a well thought out response.

 **Tips!**

- Remain positive
- Take your time
- Apply your knowledge of your current aircraft type and apply it to your answer.
- Break your answer down, keep it simple.
- Use reasoning and logic in constructing your answer.

Example:

"Describe to us the new Airbus A370 fuel system"

"OK, I haven't had the opportunity as yet to fly the A370 but I will give it a go, Being that the A370 is an ultra long range twin engine aircraft capable of flying up to 19 hours I would imagine it would have a fuel capacity in the vicinity of 160 tonnes (nineteen hours plus one hour of reserve at say eight tonnes an hour), two wing tanks plus a centre wing tank minimum, at least one stage of fuel/ oil heat exchanger and would be delivered pressurized to the engines"

"OK, anything else"

"Yes, there would certainly be a cross feed system, a jettison system and a fuel management system"

Do Not:

- Justify your lack of knowledge of the aircraft or systems
- Be embarrassed to have a go.

5. YOUR COMMAND POTENTIAL

"You have a tyre blow out just before V1, what are your actions?"

Here they are looking for your command potential and your overall thought process.

For more information refer to Chapter 9, Scenario Base Questions.

Notes

_____

_____

_____

NOTES

5. HOW TO ANSWER THE QUESTIONS

> **Your answers must be well thought out and delivered in a clear, concise and positive manner!**

THE THREE MOST IMPORTANT QUESTIONS

1. "Can you tell us about yourself?"

2. "What attributes will you bring to this company?"

3. "Why do you want to work for our company?"

These are three questions that **must and will** be asked in any panel interview. They are also the three answers that you must perform well with in order to be a successful candidate.

QUESTION 1. CAN YOU TELL US ABOUT YOURSELF?

- ■ "Tell us about yourself" OR
- ■ "Tell us about your career to date"? OR
- ■ "Tell us how you got to be sitting here today"?

This question is normally the interview opener.

"Nice to meet you Mark, why don't you start by telling us a little bit about yourself?"

Some may call it an "ice breaker" but in reality it sets the tone for the remainder of the interview.

Your answer must highlight and concentrate primarily on your aviation career, you are there for an aviation position so keep it aviation related.

Your answer should be more than just a repeat of your C.V.

Structure your answer using the following guidelines;

- ■ Start off with a quick introduction of yourself, your interests and the current position you hold.
- ■ Then go all the way back to the beginning of your interest in aviation, how you went about achieving your licences and ratings, leading into your first job and subsequent career.

- When you mention each position and job, talk about what you learnt and your experiences there. Try to keep it brief avoiding long, drawn out stories. Accentuate the positives of your time at the company.

- Bring your story to a close with a brief but strong summary of your current position and employment.. This is referred to as closing the "loop".

- Finally, finish off with a statement such as "I am ready to take the next step in my career and are very excited about this opportunity today"

"My name is Jason Stevens, I am 28 years old, married and the father of two young girls. I am a keen fisherman and enjoy keeping fit by cycling and chasing my girls around the backyard.
I am currently employed as a Dash 8 First Officer with Central Plains Airlines. I remember from a very young age I always wanted to be a pilot. So when I graduated, I worked full time in a factory to save up enough money to start my Commercial Licence. I also took out a personal loan, which I have almost paid off. This enabled me to enroll in a full time course. I completed my commercial license in 2002 at Proflite Flying School in California and was immediately employed as a flight instructor. I really enjoyed instructing, not only did I get to hone my skills but it was such a pleasure to see my students evolve into pilots, the highlight was always sending them first solo. In late 2004, after 2 years of instructing I had just over 1000hrs, so I decided it was time to look at expanding my experience. Fortunately enough I was offered a fantastic position with Phoenix Air Charter. This involved relocating to Phoenix to take up a First Officer position on a Brasilia. Unfortunately shortly after my initial line check the company went into liquidation. I found myself out of work, so in order to support my family undertook casual waiting jobs at night whilst job hunting by day. Throughout this time I maintained my motivation and never gave up. In December 2006 I was offered and accepted a position with Central Plains Airlines in Arizona on the Metroliner and worked my way up to the position of First Officer on the Dash 8-400. I have been with Central Plains Airlines for just over 4 years now, throughout this time I have enjoyed learning the airline way and specifically the multi crew operations. I now have just over 4000hrs total with 2600 hrs on turbo props. I feel I am ready for the next challenge in my career and am very excited to have this opportunity today with your airline."

It is essential to rehearse this answer, however it must come over as fresh, interesting and unscripted. The best way to achieve this is by keeping the manner and grammar of your answer informal, as if you are chatting to a friend over coffee. It needs to come from the heart and have your **passion** and **enthusiasm** shine through.

Stories about your time in a particular company will keep the panel interested as well as making your answer personal to you.

The importance of this is that when the company has the "wash up" of all the interviewees for the week they will review the notes on your particular interview. You want to stand out through keeping your answers interesting, not by a scripted, perfectly worded answer that is impersonal.

Try an example for yourself

_____

_____

_____

_____

_____

_____

_____

_____

_____

Try to create a hook in your answer. This is something the interviewers will remember you by. Unfortunately most candidates tend to blend into one another after long days of interviewing. If you can add in an interesting story or fact about yourself, this will give them something to remember you by. "the guy that grew up in Kenya", "the guy that use to look after a camel heard in Australia." The guy that use to work at that Tequila factory putting those little red hats on the bottles." "The girl that use to drive 3 hours each way to go to her flying lessons on the weekends". Hooks make you memorable and create an anchor for the interviewers to fall back on.

When you discuss employment at a previous company always talk about the positives of your time there. If you find that you had difficultly in certain positions and times in your career the less said the better. Keep it brief and positive.

"It was challenging, I learnt a lot from my time there."

If for some reason you left a company on unhappy terms, there is no need to go into to much detail , in fact there is no need to mention why you left.

"After 8 months I then had accumulated just over 1000hrs total and I was really looking at consolidating my instrument flying and building my experience in charter and multi-engine flying. After a short time canvassing my preferred companies I was fortunate enough to be offered employment with...

You didn't mention the negatives of why you moved on, you also didn't lie about it, you just left it out and concentrated on the positives of how you moved forward with your career.

If you were fired or let go from a position, please refer to our chapter on "The F Word".

Remember, everything is **positive**, all is good, you are an **upbeat** and **happy** person with a fantastic outlook on life! If this persona is displayed then this is how the interviewers will remember you. If you come across as a negative person who has had a hard career and feels hard done by, then the interviewers will go away with a negative outlook on your performance and will certainly think twice about employing someone with those characteristics.

Interviewers remember negative statements. Avoid using "I can't" I don't" or "I haven't", instead tell them you what you are willing to do or try and what you are looking forward to. Always end on a positive. If you haven't flown a twin aircraft or operated multi-crew, say "When the opportunity presents itself I am ready and I am very much looking forward to it." Isn't that better than saying. "I haven't flown multi-crew yet." or "I don't get to fly the twins, I'm too junior."

If you have areas of non-aviation employment then by all means mention it, however keep it brief. For example:

"From 2002 to 2004 I was employed in various IT positions for two major communications companies based out of Sydney."

 **Tips!**

- Talk slowly and emphasis the important information.
- Be sincere, passionate and positive!
- Don't waffle or repeat yourself, keep it short and to the point. Thorough yet succinct.
- Be clear, concise whilst using positive words.
- Never make a personal comment or opinion on someone or something.
- Add in short examples of your time in particular companies
- Remember your posture, it's not just what you say but how you say it.
- Be familiar with yourself, your work experience and the skills you bring to the table. Match these with the position and organisation you are interviewing for.
- Don't talk and waste time on irrelevant skills, certificates and experience, leave that information to the resume.
- Use positive body language, don't shift in your seat, or cross your arms, it states nervousness and disinterest.
- Be focused and pay attention to what is going on, having a good response to the questions being asked is crucial.

QUESTION 2. WHAT ATTRIBUTES WILL YOU BRING TO THIS COMPANY?

Other variations of this question can be:

- What attributes will you be bringing with you?
- Why should we hire you?
- How do you stand out amongst the other candidates?
- How would your current manager describe you?
- What are your strengths?
- How would your best friend describe you?
- How do you see yourself helping our organization?
- What do you have to offer over and above the other candidates we are interviewing today?

This question is all about you and this is your moment to ...

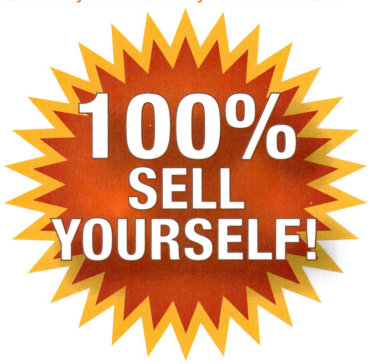

There is a simple method to follow that helps anyone to answer this question. The best way to start is to write down 5 descriptive words that best describe you. Expanding the words into examples.

Below are some descriptive words to get you started.

Motivated	Passionate	Show initiative	Driven
Hard working	Positive	Respectful	Team Player
Focused	Responsible	Energetic	Enthusiastic
Calm	Approachable	Professional	Unfazed
Composed	Gentle	Active	Honest
Reliable	Dedicated	Flexible	Friendly
Integrity	Loyal	Patient	Relaxed
Emphatic	Leadership	Communicator	

1. _____

2. _____

3. _____

4. _____

5. _____

What do you have to offer our company?

"I am DEDICATED to my career, I worked part time in the hospitality industry for over three years in order to support my passion for flying and to allow myself to pursue my career in aviation. On completion of my commercial pilots licence I packed my bags and headed North to Darwin in hope of finding work. After 3 months of cleaning hangars I was offered my first charter flight with the company. I was told it was in reward for my hard work and dedication. I stayed with that company for over 3 years, during which time I moved up through the ranks until I was flying RPT multi-crew operations on the metroliner.

I am also very RELIABLE. I am more than happy to help out in anyway that I can and my company know that they can always rely on me. Recently the company found themselves short staffed at the last minute so they called me on a day off, I was in the pre-flight briefing within the hour. In the past I have also helped out with extensions of duty when requested.

I am very PASSIONATE about my flying career, from a very young age I have loved aviation. I still to this day collect model aircraft and am always excited to go to work and never think of it as a chore. I wear my uniform with pride and I am always striving to do the best job possible on every flight.

*I am also very HONEST and APPROACHABLE. I am not afraid to admit fault, own up to a problem or speak up if I feel I need to. I believe my honesty and positive outlook on life also makes me more approachable. In the past I have often found myself being approached by the "new guy" who has numerous questions about our operation and I am more than happy to sit down and go over things to help out in my spare time. This is what I have to offer Virtual Airlines."

DESCRIPTION PLUS EVIDENCE GIVES CREDIBILITY

Now that you have your 5 descriptive words and your examples, lets have a look at the method we use to answer the various questions you can be faced with. We want to make this easy for you, we want you to be able to use this one answer and mold it to suit the different questions that you may be faced with.

There can be over 10 questions asked where you can utilize this one answer. How we do this? We use the Question to our advantage, we take key words from the question and add them into our answer and adjust our answer to suit.

Have a look at the examples below.

"How would your current manager describe you?"

"My current manager, Mr Peter Smith would describe me as a very dedicated person, he knows the hard work and dedication I have put into my career, he has over the years rewarded me for my hard work by allowing me to continually upgrade within the company, where am currently a captain on the metroliner, the largest aircraft in our fleet.

Mr Smith would also describe me as reliable, he can rely on me to get the job done without supervision and can call on me anytime should they find themselves short staffed with a flight to be completed.

He would also say that I am very passionate about aviation, he sees me coming to work looking very professional and proud to be part of the company.

I am very honest and approachable, I am not afraid to admit fault, own up to a problem or speak up if I feel I need to. He prefers to pass the new recruits onto me too nurture and train.

"This is how I believe Mr Smith would describe me."

See how I used the question to open and close my answer as well as using key words in the question throughout my answer.

Again:

What would you say are 3 of your strengths.

"I would say my first strength would be my dedication to my career and job. I worked part time......... etc

My second strength I would say is my ability to be reliable, I am more than happy to help out......... etc

And my final strength I would say is my ability to be honest and approachable. I am not afraid to ....etc"

Q "How do you see yourself contributing to our organization?"

*"I see myself **contributing to your organization** through the following attributes. I am very hardworking and dedicated to the company I work for, this attribute has enabled me to move up quickly within my current company, I strive to be the best pilot I can be.*

*I also see myself **contributing** through my reliability. I am more than happy to help the company out on days off, I am often the pilot called when the company is short staffed and I am more than happy to extend my duty when required in order to get the job done.*

I am also very passionate and I bring professionalism to the work place, wearing my uniform with pride and being aware that I am the face of the company.

I have a positive outlook and attitude. For this reason I am tasked with inducting the new recruits into our organization.

*I know I will fit in well with the people you employ and **contribute** with a positive attitude and willingness to learn and grow within your organization."*

Know your opening and closing statements well enough to make them powerful!

QUESTION 3. WHY DO YOU WANT TO WORK FOR OUR AIRLINE?

The answer should be 90% about the company and only 10% about you.

There are two great resources to help you on your way.

- Visit the Airlines website. Click on "About Us". Here you will find details on such things as the companies "ethos", headquarters, personnel, destinations etc. This is a handy insight into how the company views itself.
- Visit Wikipedia and search for your airline. Print it out and make notes to refer back too.

After having researched the company you then need to build your answer. A simple way to structure your answer is to create 3 points.

1. **About the company; How you personally view the company, anything that links you personally to the company it's reputation in the industry, financial state, growth, awards and any extra information that is key to the company operation. Be honest here.**

2. **The Aircraft they fly, the type of operation and their destinations. Why that interests you, now and for the future.**

3. **The people they employ, the lifestyle and the opportunity for you as a pilot.**

Simplifying it to 3 points and then personalising it by stating why these facts are important to you is the key. Let's have a look at an example below.
Please note that the facts contained in the below example are fictional, please don't quote this information in your interview.

(1) "The very first aeroplane I ever went on was a Cathay Pacific B747 from Hong Kong to London during a family holiday. Since that day I have always thought of Cathay as the premium airline and a company I would love to fly for one day".

(2) "Cathay Pacific is a company that has consistently shown financial strength in the market, just last year the annual profit was $14B, up 30% from last year. This is important to me because it will offer me job security. Cathay Pacific has also won many awards for excellence over the years, consistently being in the top 3 Skytracks awards for "Airline of the year". The pilots are regarded as the best trained in the industry and are hugely respected. I have always wanted to be the best pilot that I can be and I would be very proud to work for Cathay Pacific.

(3) You fly a variety of aircraft, from the latest B777-300ER to the A330 and have over 90 aircraft currently on order, you are also about to take delivery of the new A350. You also boast one of the youngest fleets in the industry. Along with this you have a variety of destinations and operations, Ultra Long Haul to regional flying. This is important to me as I consider Cathay as a career move, an airline I will stay with for the rest of my career, You will give me fantastic aircraft to fly, variety of flying, keeping me interested and challenged throughout my career.

(4) The type of people you employ are friendly, young, professional and from all ends of the globe, a true international company. I know I will enjoy going to work everyday. Cathay will also offer me a lifestyle change that I will embrace, the chance to live in Hong Kong. It is for these reason I would very much like to work for Cathay Pacific."

Make notes on the following.

Company headquarters and key personnel

_____

_____

_____

_____

Brief History

_____

_____

_____

_____

Financial situation, business outlook and management style

_____

_____

_____

_____

Alliances

_____

_____

_____

_____

Aircraft type, numbers and orders

_____

_____

_____

_____

Destinations, frequency and future destinations

_____

_____

_____

_____

Key markets i.e. business, leisure etc

_____

_____

_____

_____

The type of people they employ

_____

_____

_____

_____

And most importantly, what makes the company unique

_____

_____

_____

_____

Having now done your research combine your information into a unique answer.

Example: Virgin Australia

A _" Virgin Australia has an innovative approach to business with a very dynamic and forward way of thinking. They have adjusted their brand and are expanding into the professional business side of the market The company has a secure financial position with recent expansions internationally into the Asia Pacific region along with the acquisition of Skywest, providing plenty of opportunity for advancement. They have a modern fleet of aircraft that are highly efficient, flying to interesting destinations around Australia and the Pacific. Everyone within the company seems to have an energy about them that is contagious, they are open, upbeat and friendly. On a personal note working for Virgin Australia would offer me a long-term stable career with boundless opportunities in an environment that is enjoyable, ever changing and one that I would be very proud to be a part of._

This answer shows:

- You have done your research.
- You respect their company.
- You are enthusiastic about working for the company.
- You can see yourself fitting into the culture of the company.

As this is a definite question, you really need to have done your homework. Once you have done your homework, then you need to sit back and ask yourself honestly "Why do I want to work for this airline". Be honest and open about it and use this as the basis to your answer backing it up with the facts you found during your homework. This way your answer will be genuine and passionate. Now create your unique answer.

Notes

6. OTHER POWERFUL QUESTIONS

"What do you hope to gain out of employment with us?"

"Where do you see yourself in 5 years?"

"What is your ultimate goal with our airline?"

"What are your expectations of working for us?"

Be honest with your answer without sounding too selfish. At any opportunity bring in the positive aspects of the company. This answer is really a combination of your answer to "why you want to work for us". Be honest with how you see your future unfolding with them.

Example

A   *"I hope to gain a long-term stable career with a company that offers a variety of flying, both domestic and international with a variety of modern jet aircraft. I hope to gain my Captaincy on the B737 and with my instructing background possibly move into a position of check and training. I would also look forward to going to work each day knowing that I would be operating with crew that are genuinely happy, friendly and professional."*

NEGATIVE STYLE QUESTIONS

Negative style questions are there to trip you up. You must be very careful not to talk about your current employment in any way that can be looked upon as negative. You could easily end up contradicting yourself from what has already been discussed in the interview.

With a little forethought, there are some very easy answers to what can appear to be extremely difficult questions.

 **Tips!**

- Show positive and confident body language.
- Be brief.
- Don't justify, just state the facts.
- Only mention one point.
- Mention only positives about the company.
- Don't act dejected.
- Short, to the point and move on.
- Just answer the question.

EXAMPLE

Q   "What don't you like about your current job?"

I am currently flying the largest aircraft in the company. I have achieved all I have set out to achieve within the company. As much as I love the company and the position, I feel now is an ideal time to move on in order to satisfy my career objectives and goals."

Q   "What would you change about the company you currently work for if you had the chance?"

For this style of question think about how you could improve the company in order to make it more efficient and effective and improve their bottom line.

1. *"I would implement a more structured rostering system, possibly a rolling four week roster, including a rotating standby system. Not only would this improve pilot morale and even out the work load, it would also increase productivity thereby creating a more efficient and effective company."*

2. *" I would consider introducing basings at two of our busiest ports. Currently we have several pilots and crew that overnight in A and B cities with the added expense of hotels, meals and transport. If we introduced basing, which I know would be a popular decision among the crew, I believe the company could make significantly savings.*

Q   "If you had a job offer from both us and XXX Airlines, which one would you choose?"

This is obviously a delicate question and one that will require a lot of thought on your behalf before the interview. Stay upbeat and positive, Here's an example.

"If I am fortunate to be offered positions with both companies I will stick to my original goal of working with Jetblue. Jetblue can offer me the opportunities to fly a range of aircraft both domestically and internationally and I believe has the right culture fit for me as a person"

Word of WARNING! Avoid at all cost any situation or answer that may be construed as being negative.

Focus on the positives of the company you are interviewing for.

Did you notice in the example above there was **NO** mention of XXX Airlines. There is no need to mention them at all.

Short, to the point and move on.

Q   "This position involves you moving country, you will be based in Hong Kong, why don't you want to live in your own country?"

"Well it's got nothing to do with not wanting to live in my own country, I love my own country, however if the opportunities for me to advance my career and fly for the company I have always dreamed of involve living in Hong Kong, I am very excited about that too."

Again, short to the point, positive and nothing said about what you DON'T WANT, everything is about what you DO want.

Another style of question:

Q   "Why don't you want to work for one of your own carriers, there is nothing wrong with them?"

Now you have a go at answering this one:

_____

_____

_____

_____

_____

_____

_____

Q   "Tell us about a time recently you have been under stress, how did you recognize it and how did you cope with it?" or "How do you cope with stress in general?"

This doesn't specifically have to be about aviation. What they are looking for is how you cope with stress in general and how you analyze problems from the past. Be honest about the problem and how it affected you without going into too much detail. Remember to add in how you cope with stress in general. Don't forget they are looking for how you recognised the stress and how you coped and then how you solved the problem. They don't care what the stressor was so you can be honest here.

Q   "A time recently when you found yourself to be stressed?"

1. "We were fast approaching an unrealistic deadline and it was clear to me that the project would not be finished to my standards in time".

2. "My wife's family were struggling financially with their business and we had a lot of money tied up with it."

3. "I accepted a new basing which came in conjunction with my upgrade to command on a new aircraft type. I had to move states, which involved renting out my own house, looking for a new house in a new city that I was unfamiliar with whilst studying for my command on a new aircraft type

Try an example for yourself.

_____

_____

_____

_____

_____

"How did you recognize it?"

- ■ I found I was lacking concentration.
- ■ I became quite irritable, people commented on my moods.
- ■ I started to lose my appetite.
- ■ I wasn't sleeping very well.
- ■ I felt like I was operating on autopilot - not really thinking.

_____

_____

_____

_____

"How did you deal with it?"

- ■ I confronted the problem head on.
- ■ I organized a plan of attack to solve the problem.
- ■ I wrote out a schedule of "must do items" in order of priority.
- ■ I admitted fault and communicated this to the appropriate people involved.
- ■ I opened up the communication lines.

_____

_____

"How do you cope with stress in general?"

- ■ I recognize the problem and make an effort to deal with it.
- ■ I spend time with my friends, go to BBQ's and take time out for myself.
- ■ I take the family dog for a walk.
- ■ I find that by going surfing and mountain bike riding I can clear my mind.
- ■ I go to the movies, read a book, meditate.
- ■ I talk with my girlfriend/ wife/ colleagues about the problem and ask for their advice, opinion.

_____

_____

_____

_____

WEAKNESSES

What is a weakness of yours?

Name three of your weaknesses?

What would you say is your biggest weakness?

What would your superior say is something you could improve on?

When you mention weaknesses you want to select those that are actually similar to your strengths, or attributes. You should structure your answer to include the following;

- What it is
- Why you believe it is a weakness
- That you are aware of it
- How you cope with it
- What you are doing about it

If you have mentioned that you are "very reliable" as one of your strengths, because you always answer the phone on days off, always extend duty when required and rarely call in sick etc. Then you can use this as a weakness.

For Example;

What it is

"I find it hard to say 'No' to people."

Why it's a weakness

"Sometimes I end up taking too much on, I don't end up getting the time to do anything for myself or/ I don't end up completing the task to the manner in which I would have liked because I didn't have the time/ or say yes to work when they call on a day off when I actually had plans with family and friends."

"I am aware of it"

What you are doing about it

"I am learning to balance my lifestyle between work and personal commitments and prioritising my time.

Other ideas for weaknesses

1. "I am a perfectionist, it tends to take me longer to complete a task as I want to do it to the best of my abilities and get it right the first time. For example, when I wash and clean one of our aircraft I tend to take around 90 minutes, most guys take about half that time, that is just me, I am aware of it and when I take on a task like that I just make sure I have to time available to do it to the standard I like to."

2. "My love and passion for aviation can also be a weakness. I tend to talk too much about aviation, I live and breath it and I know this can annoy those close to me. I am aware of it, so I do try to make an effort to limit my talk of aviation, or at least keep my aviation talk contained within the work environment only."

3. "I am very open and honest. Sometimes I tend to engage my mouth before my brain. Sometimes this can come across as rude or insensitive, when I certainly never intended it to be so. I am known for calling a spade a spade. I am aware of it, so now I slow down and make sure I think about things before I open my mouth!"

4. "With my carefree and positive happy go lucky attitude I tend to lose things. I get so caught up in the moment with either work or friends that when I leave a place I just simply forget things like my keys, or mobile phone. Gosh, the number of phones I have left in taxi's!! I am certainly aware of it and I now make a conscious effort to check that I have those items before I move on."

5. "I am very trusting. I have found in the past that I have been taken advantage of because of this. I have lent money to friends, never to see it again. I am learning to say no and to trust my instincts."

6. "I don't have the best paperwork skills and my handwriting could be a lot better" etc.

7. "I don't have the best long term memory. I'm lucky as I pick up things really quickly, however I tend to forget them after a certain amount of time. What I now do is keep my study up every 6 months and make sure I review certain things, this seems to work well for me."

Notes

OVERCOMING NEGATIVES AND THE 'F' WORD

Most of us at some point in our careers have had extended periods of unemployment, been let go of, left a job on bad terms, or even been fired. Everyone has some form of skeleton in their closet, including those who are conducting the interview!

The important thing is how you deal with it in under the pressure of an interview. If you go into the interview carrying baggage from a previous situation the interviewers will most certainly pick up on it and probe deeper until your true feelings are exposed for the world to see. It is essential that you deal with the issue before the interview, you need to turn the negative incident into a positive outcome.

1. Periods of unemployment.

If you have had extended periods of unemployment highlight positively how you filled your time.

"During the downturn of 2008 I found myself unemployed for a period of six months. Whilst still actively job hunting I filled in my extra time by starting a fitness regime of cycling, swimming and yoga. For mental stimulation every Friday I worked as a volunteer at the local school library."

2. Leaving on unhappy terms or being asked to resign.

There are two ways you can approach this and that depends on the job you secure after this event.

a) If there was a backwards step from this position or you are actually in this position then you will have to approach it in this manner.

"I found myself in a position where I simply did not see eye to eye with the Chief Pilot and the style of operation the company was conducting. It was extremely hard to walk away from the position, however it taught me a lot about myself and my values. It also gave me the opportunity to reflect back on what is important to me in the work place and I believe I am a better person for the experience. I then managed to find work with Aviation Airlines where initially I was flying the ...."

b) If it was some time ago in your career and you actually went to a job that was a step up, then you can approach it in this manner when talking about why you left this particular company and position.

" After working with XXX company for 4 months I was offered a fantastic opportunity with XXX company, one which I couldn't refuse ...

Now you haven't lied, you just haven't offered up or gone into the detail of exactly what happened and there really is no need to either. However if for any reason they question you directly about this or ask for further detail, DO NOT LIE about what happened. Explain it as in the above example.

When addressing negative questions it is best to keep the information to a minimum, short and to the point. Don't labour the situation, you will sound like you are making excuses and that you are trying to convince the interview team of your point of view, this can only lead to a negative outcome.

S A S

SUMMARISE AND STOP

3. Being Fired.

COPING WITH THE "F" WORD IN AN INTERVIEW.

You would be surprised to know that there are a lot more pilot's out there that have been Fired other than yourself, including, most probably one or two of those sitting on the interview panel.

The problem is of course, you are the one being interviewed so how are you going to deal with it?

I know through personal experience what It is like to be fired and there are quiet a few emotions you will go through, but there is light at the end of the tunnel if you follow a few simple tips.

First of all the emotions will probably involve;

Disbelief and Blame

"I can't believe they have done this to me, surely when they know the whole story I will get my job back, it wasn't' really my fault."

Or maybe it was your fault but you feel that all the hard work previous to the incident will prove it was just out of character for you and you have been harshly dealt with or made an example of.

Realisation and Shame

This has really happened, how am I going to tell my family and friends, I just want to hide under a rock and never come out.

Now What?

"How am I ever going to get another job, how am I ever going to explain this in an interview, who would want to hire me? Have I ruined forever my chances of a career?"

It is all up to you now, the key is knowing how to turn this negative event in your career into a positive event.

Tell It How It Is.

Don't even think about telling half truths either, simply tell the truth, without emotion or too much detail, just the facts and then STOP.

This way you display credibility, integrity and responsibility.

Tell Them On Your Terms

The first instant you get to tell what happened take it! Normally most interviews open with "Andrew it's nice to meet you, why don't you start by telling us about yourself and your career to date."

There is your opportunity to explain, on your own terms and in the comfort of a "learnt" answer, this event in your career.

Blame.

You simply cannot go into an interview and blame someone else for your actions. The only person to blame is yourself, It wasn't your boss, the aircraft, the operation etc.

This may take a while to get your head around but the reality is, you are the only one to blame here. The sooner you realise this, the sooner you can get back into the workforce. Try to look at it objectively and avoid emotion here, again stick to facts and keep emotions at bay.

Be Accountable

OK, so you have accepted the blame now it is time to take responsibility and look back at how and why things went wrong. Accepting and learning from this is the key. However you can achieve this, be it through talking to close friends, meditation, long walks, time out and even therapy. You need to find peace with this.

Do not be ashamed. You will find the more you talk about this, the quicker you get over it. It happened, how you deal with it will determine whether or not you get through the interview. Again, if it is not a problem for you, it won't be a problem for them. You may be surprised to know that in the end most people don't really even care that you were fired.

The Story

What exactly do you say, how much detail do I go into, how do I explain what happened?

Be concise and to the point, leave emotions behind. They will not expect a detailed account of what happened and you should not offer them one.

SUMMARISE AND STOP

Moving Forward

It is REALLY important that you are able to explain what you learnt from the experience and is a nice way to end. This may include what you learnt about yourself as well as how you would behave should the situation arise in the future.

"Personally I have learnt the importance of communication in the workforce, particularly aviation. I have looked back on my communication style during the event, realized I could have handled the situation better and have taken steps to ensure I communicate more effectively in the future"

Notice how I have explained this in a positive way, taken responsibility, learnt and moved on.

Practice

It is essential to practice and rehearse your answer, to anyone who will listen and ask them to be objective.

"Would you hire me after that?"

The more comfortable and confident you are talking about it in a professional manner the more likely it is you will gain the respect of the panel.

Now for an example;

As mentioned above, try to explain things the first chance you get, don't go into the detail, however mention it and move on to more positive things, have a look at the example below which would be part of your answer to "Tell us about yourself and your career to date?"

"...during my time with XXX company I enjoyed a variety of flying. I very much enjoyed the challenge of the weather and conditions in the area, it was great experience and I learnt a few valuable lessons during my time there. After 18 months and approximately 900 hrs of flying I had an incident which resulted in the termination of my employment...

(Here you can explain in point form what happened-briefly stating facts)

...I take full responsibility for what happened and I understand the companies decision. Of course I was very disappointed and initially quite shocked at what had happened however I decided to turn the situation into a learning experience. I decided to take the opportunity to update my CV and complete my ATPL's (or gain a new type rating/ endorsement etc) while apply to as many companies and positions as possible. I looked for work that would give me challenges, new experiences and further my career in a positive way. I also took on board what happened in my previous employment, I learnt from that experience and decided I would not allow myself to be in that situation ever again. Fortunately within two months I was offered a position with XXX in the role of .... Flying.....aircraft..." etc

Notes

_____

_____

_____

_____

_____

_____

_____

_____

_____

_____

_____

_____

_____

_____

_____

_____

_____

_____

_____

_____

7. BEHAVIOURAL QUESTIONS

TELL US ABOUT A TIME ...?

These type of questions are known as behavioral questions and the theory, rightly or wrongly is that how you have behaved, reacted, managed, conducted yourself in the past is an indication of how you will behave in the future. They are a feature of the modern job interview and can be quite daunting to the unprepared.

Behavioral questions generally fall into three categories.

1. Example Based Questions

2. Negative or Difficult Questions

3. Open Ended Questions

In preparation for these questions we recommend putting together a list of at least five scenarios that you have **PERSONALLY** been Involved with. They **must** be aviation related. Once you have thought out and planned your examples you can adapt them to virtually any question that is thrown your way.

If the interview is purely based on behavioral questions (No Technical questions) it is advised to come up with at least eight scenarios.

The following areas must be covered;

- Planning, working to a deadline
- Teamwork
- Conflict
- Communication
- Error making and recovery
- Bending or breaking rules
- Thinking on the spot
- Being assertive

Write down a short example for the following.

1.   When have you been involved with a task that had a deadline?
(Hint; ATPL's or aircraft conversions are good for this example.)

_____

_____

_____

_____

2.   An occasion when you worked successfully in a team environment.
(Hint; A team can consist of yourself, ground staff, loaders and other crew members.)

_____

_____

_____

_____

3.   A time you have had difficulty working with a colleague?
(Hint; Be honest, say what was difficult, don't offer excuses, end on how you dealt with it.)

_____

_____

_____

_____

4. When you had to change your communication style to suit your audience.

(Hint; Someone where English was their second language, or a non aviation person.)

_____

_____

_____

_____

_____

_____

5. When have you have not performed to your manager's expectations?

(Hint; This should be early on in your career when mistakes are expected to be made).

_____

_____

_____

_____

Now that you have your examples, when structuring your answers follow this three-part process using the acronym:

S. A. O

S = The situation. You must explain the situation in detail. When (time frame), What (you were flying) Where (you were flying) and Who you were with. The more detail you give the better for them to understand the Actions you took.

A = The Actions. The actions and options you come up with are the key. The really don't care about the situation, how bad it was, what they care about are the actions you took and the options you came up with in order to get yourself out of the situation.

O = The Outcome. This can include a basic summary of what happened in the end, however it may also include what you learnt in the process that has now built you to be the person and pilot that you are today.

This may seem easy, but it's not! What can tend to happen here is we get so caught up in telling our story, by the end of it we have completely forgotten what the question is and the interviewers are wondering if you even answered the question!

So to avoid this happening to you in the interview we have a simple method use to answer these style of questions.

USE THE QUESTION TO YOUR ADVANTAGE

USE THE QUESTION TO YOUR ADVANTAGE.

It's that simple.

Open with the question, repeat the question throughout your answer and end with the question.

This helps you in two ways, it helps keep you on track and makes sure you answer the question as well as highlighting to the interviewers that you are actually answering the question.

If the question is quite long, then just use key words.

One thing to note, at anytime when answering questions and you get to the end of your answer and you are not sure how to end, to avoid " ah, well , um yeh so that's about it." All you need to do is repeat the question.

" They are the main reasons why I want to work for your company."

" So they are three of my strengths."

" That is definitely my biggest weakness."

" That is a time when I really had to act quickly on my feet."

Your answers can be quite involved, don't be surprised if you end up talking for around three minutes.

At the end of your examples and when practicing make sure at the end of it all that you check you have actually answered the question and not just told a great story! Did you even remember what the question was?

Sometimes you may have to make a brief introduction to your story before you dive straight into the Situation.

For Example; "A time you had to act quickly on your feet?"

"Yes I had to act quickly on my feet recently when I had a gear problem in my aircraft when I was on approach to land, now it was about three months ago…"

"Give an example of a time you had to act quickly on your feet?"

The Situation

A time I had to act quickly on my feet was about 3 months ago when I was operating a charter flight from Moree to Brisbane in a Cessna 310 with four passengers on board. On reaching the circuit area and lowering the landing gear I received both visual and oral cues that the left gear was not fully extended.

The Action Taken

I had to act quickly on my feet so I silenced the warning horn by retracting the flaps, which both calmed the passengers and allowed me to focus on the task at hand. I decided to hold 5nm away from the circuit to give me more time to go through the checklist. I actioned the appropriate checklist which included manually extending the landing gear. This gave me the required three green lights indicating the gear was down and locked. To further confirm the gear was down I requested a fly by of the tower. After confirmation by the tower I extended the landing flaps to ensure there was no warning horn.

The Outcome

I completed my landing checklist and made a normal approach and landing. On disembarking the group leader commented on my calm demeanor and professionalism during a tense situation. So that would be a time I can say that I had to act quickly on my feet.

Got it? Great, now try for yourself.

Describe a time you used logic to solve an unusual situation?

The Situation

_____

_____

_____

_____

_____

_____

_____

_____

Your Actions

_____

_____

_____

_____

_____

_____

_____

_____

The Outcome

_____

_____

_____

_____

_____

Describe to us a time you led a team to a successful outcome?

The Situation

_____

_____

_____

_____

_____

_____

_____

_____

_____

Your Actions

_____

_____

_____

_____

_____

_____

_____

_____

The Outcome

_____

_____

_____

_____

_____

_____

Tell us about a time you have had a personal conflict with a work colleague?

The Situation

_____

_____

_____

_____

_____

_____

_____

Your Actions

_____

_____

_____

_____

_____

_____

_____

The Outcome

_____

_____

_____

_____

_____

_____

_____

When have you had to change your communication style to get your point across?

The Situation

_____

_____

_____

_____

_____

_____

_____

Your Actions

_____

_____

_____

_____

_____

_____

The Outcome

_____

_____

_____

_____

_____

_____

_____

Tell us about a time your performance was lacking? How did you recognize it and what did you do to resolve the situation?

The Situation

_____

_____

_____

_____

_____

_____

_____

Your Actions

_____

_____

_____

_____

_____

_____

_____

_____

The Outcome

_____

_____

_____

_____

_____

More examples of behavioral question you should be prepared for.

- Describe a situation in which you were able to use persuasion to successfully convince someone to see things your way.
- Describe a time when you were faced with a stressful situation that demonstrated your coping skills.
- Give me a specific example of a time when you used good judgment and logic in solving a problem.
- Give me an example of a time when you set a goal and were able to meet or achieve it.
- Tell me about a time when you had to use your presentation skills to influence someone's opinion.
- Give me a specific example of a time when you had to conform to a policy with which you did not agree with.
- Tell me about a time in flight when you felt under pressure.
- Tell me about a time you had to do a monotonous task, how did you keep motivated.
- Tell me about a time when you had to go above and beyond the call of duty in order to get a job done.
- Tell me about a time when you had too many things to do and you were required to prioritize your tasks.
- Give me an example of a time when you had to make a split second decision.
- What is your typical way of dealing with conflict? Give me an example.
- Tell me about a time you were able to successfully deal with another person even when that individual may not have personally liked you (or vice versa).
- Tell me about a difficult decision you've made in the last year.
- Give me an example of a time when something you tried to accomplish had failed.
- Give me an example of when you showed initiative.
- Tell me about a recent situation in which you had to deal with a very upset customer or co-worker.
- Give me an example of a time when you motivated others.
- Tell me about a time when you lost situation awareness.
- Give me an example of a time when you used your fact-finding skills to solve a problem.
- Tell me about a time when you missed an obvious solution to a problem.
- Describe a time when you anticipated potential problems and developed preventive measures.
- Tell me about a time when you were forced to make an unpopular decision.
- Please tell me about a time you had to fire someone you were fond of.
- Describe a time when you set your sights too high (or too low).
- A time you had to complete a task that was well below your skill level, how did you keep motivated?
- A problem on the aircraft for which there were no Standard Operating Procedures to follow.
- A time you had to deal with a change in your work environment. (Think of seasonal weather, change of basing, change of management or SOPS;
- What is the longest duty you have had and how did you prepare for it.
- Tell me about a time you had to be flexible around a standard operating procedure in order to get the hob done.
- Tell me about a situation you were faced with that had multiple solutions, which one would you choose and why? (Think of needing to divert, hold or return to base due weather at destination or return to the bay for technical reasons with options of 1. Change aircraft or 2. Offload pax while fixing the problem or keep pax on board while solving the problem).

Notes

8. TECHNICAL QUESTIONS

Most airlines will ask technical questions during the interview. The types of questions will range from Instrument Flight Rules, General Aeronautical Knowledge, Meteorology, and Aerodynamics etc.

The best information available on these questions will be found in your own notes and manuals as well as forums or pilot chat websites. As the range of technical questions is vast it is not the intention of this work booklet to provide answers to all the questions but to provide you with guidance on how to structure your answers and what the interviewers are looking for.

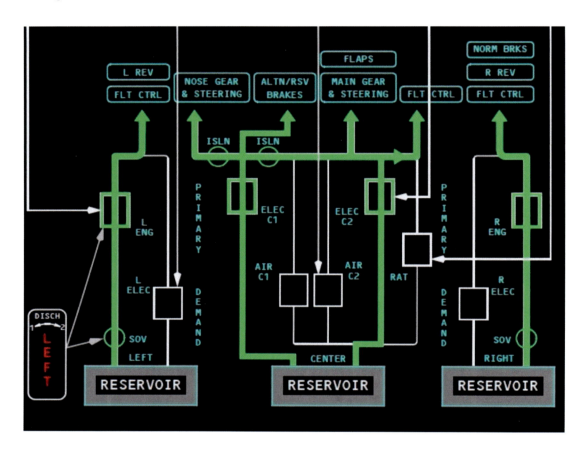

You will be asked questions on your current aircraft type, routes and destinations you serve. Be sure you study up on these items.

For international airlines you will find they are unable to ask any Local Flight Rules and Regulation questions. Only when you are applying for a local company will these questions be applicable.

For straight forward technical questions make sure you respect the interviewer and just answer the question.

For example:

Q "what is the missed approach climb gradient?"

A "2.5%"

HOW TO ANSWER OPEN ENDED TECHNICAL QUESTIONS

For Open Ended questions be mindful not to talk too much, try to get the interview to guide you through your answer by their questions. If you are asked to explain something, give a brief description and then STOP, wait for the interviewer to ask further questions on the topic. You may find they are happy with your clear and concise answer and wish to move on.

When structuring your answers be sure to keep your response short and to the point. Don't allow yourself the opportunity to get confused and tangled up. If the interviewer requires more detail let them ask for it.

This is an open-ended question (those that ask you to explain something).

Q   "Describe to us what TCAS is?"

A   *"TCAS is an acronym for Traffic Collision Avoidance System. It provides coordinated manoeuvers to the pilots of aircraft that are transponder equipped in order to avoid a collision usually within high density airports".*

Now wait for the interviewer to ask further questions.

Q   What would your action be if you had an Resolution Advisory?

Q   What would you say to ATC?

Another example.

Q   Why do some aircraft have winglets?

A   *"Winglets reduce drag by preventing the mixing of the upper and lower airflow"*

Q   What type of drag does it reduce?

A   *"Induced Drag"*

Q   OK, When is induced drag at its greatest?

A   *"During Take Off & Landing"*

This is a far better way to structure your answer and avoid confusion than,

A   *"Some aircraft have winglets to reduce drag by preventing the mixing of the upper and lower airflow therefore reducing wingtip vortices therefore reducing induced drag resulting in decreased fuel burn and therefore increase range. Induced drag is at its highest during take off and landing BLAH, BLAH, BLAH"*

GET THE IDEA?

When answering open ended questions we can't stress enough that you keep your answer brief. Answer as if you are explaining the topic to someone who has no aviation experience. The idea is that you answer the question in brief and expect the interviewer to ask further questions, therefore helping to guide you through your answer.

Some of the topics that can be asked have so much depth to them that it is hard to know where to start and finish and therefore can open up the opportunity of digging yourself into a hole!

One more example;

"What is GPWS?

"GPWS stands for Ground Proximity Warning System. It is a system built into the aircraft in order to aid the pilots to avoid Controlled Flight into Terrain".

How many alert modes are there?

"It consists of seven modes all of which have a voice announcement to bring the pilots attention to the immediate threat. Such as 'Terrain, Pull Up'."

Ok, What is enhanced GPWS?

"Enhanced GPWS uses a built in terrain database which combined with GPS allows the system to look forward rather than just vertically as is the case with traditional GPWS, ultimately giving the pilot's more time to react."

Explain the fuel system of an Airbus 340?

_____

_____

_____

_____

_____

_____

_____

_____

_____

_____

_____

_____

_____

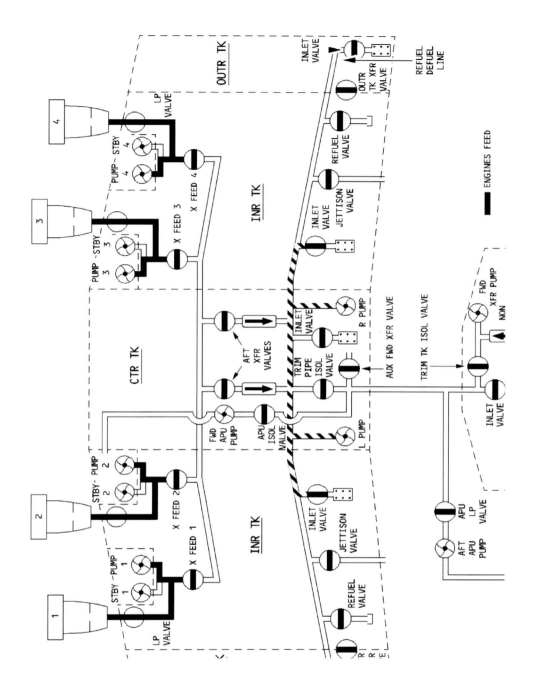

You may also be faced with technical questions that you feel are beyond your knowledge base. Such as "Can you explain to us what you know about the B777 fuel system?"

As stated in Chapter 4 use your knowledge from your ATPL study along with information from your current aircraft and apply it here. If you think about it, your aircraft fuel system isn't that different to the B777, its probably just smaller with less parts. However, I am sure it would still have tanks, pumps, vents, crossfeed, indications, warnings and possibly transfer etc.

So don't be turned off by what initially may seem like and impossible question, take your time and have a go by applying what you do know to the situation and question at hand.

Example:

Q "Describe to us the new Airbus A370 fuel system"

A *"OK, I haven't had the opportunity as yet to fly the A370 but I will give it a go. Being that the A370 is an ultra long range twin engine aircraft capable of flying up to 19 hours I would imagine it would have a fuel capacity in the vicinity of 160 tonnes (nineteen hours plus one hour of reserve at say eight tonnes an hour), two wing tanks plus a centre wing tank minimum, at least one stage of fuel/ oil heat exchanger and would be delivered pressurized to the engines, I would think it would have crossfeed and possibly transfer between tanks."*

Q "OK, anything else"

A *"Yes, there may be a jettison system and I'm sure there would be a fuel management system"*

Do Not:

- Justify your lack of knowledge of the aircraft or systems
- Be embarrassed to have a go.

SCENARIO STYLE TECHNICAL QUESTIONS

Q "You have a tyre blow out just before V1, what are your actions?"

Here they are looking for your command potential and your overall thought process.

DO you take it into the air or abort on the ground and why? Then what are your actions? How do you prioritise.

If you currently fly a high capacity aircraft then you should revert back to your current companies operating procedures.

However, If you are coming from a low flying hours background or no experience then you will have to think on your feet and look at the overall problem and prioritise. There is no right or wrong for someone with little experience when faced with this question, it is a matter of systematically working through it.

Q " You are flying your current aircraft our of your home base, after take off you suffer and engine failure. You are unable to return to the field do to poor weather, what will you do, where will you go and why?"

Again they are looking for your command potential and your overall thought process.

AVIATE

NAVIGATE

COMMUNICATE

- Secure the aircraft, running through your normal emergency procedures
- Navigate the aircraft to your selected airport. Explain your logic in the airport selection.
  - Terrain en-route and in the area, should you suffer further emergencies.
  - Familiarity with the airport, have you been there before.
  - Aids at the airport considering weather, ILS or VOR approach, are you sure you will get in and avoid a missed approach situation.
  - Passenger facilities on the ground, is it a port used by your company, will you have ground support.
  - Engineering facilities on the ground to fix the problem and minimise delay and cost to your company.
- Communicate to ATC, your company if possible and your passengers.

Notes

SAMPLE TECHNICAL QUESTIONS

- Why do aircraft have swept wings, what are the advantages?
- What is induced drag?
- How can we reduce induced drag?
- Why do aircraft have winglets?
- Why doesn't' the B777 have winglets?
- What happens to the stall speed as load factor increases?
- How is Dutch Roll prevented on the B777?
- Is the yaw damper in parallel or series?
- What type of reversers does the B747 have?
- Does the core of the engine still produce Fwd thrust during reverse?
- What happens to your Mach No as you climb at a constant IAS?
- What is the definition of Angle Of Attack.
- Draw the Lift curve for us? Why did you stop the curve there?
- What is the lift formula?
- What changes rho (air density)?
- How does weight effect the stalling angle?
- How is Mach No calculated?
- How does temperature effect Mach No?
- In regards to Auto-Land, what is the difference between fail operational and fail passive?
- Explain what you know about the B747 fuel system?
- Why does it have fuel in the tail, what is the tank called?
- What is the fuel tank in the tail of the A330/A340 called and why is it called that?
- What is the difference between carbon and steel brakes?
- How does a typhoon form?
- What is the main difference between a typhoon and a cyclone?
- Does sea depth effect the formation of a typhoon?
- If we were in Singapore would a typhoon form there?
- Describe a cold front?
- What would a warm front look like if you were flying towards it?
- What is the transponder code for a radio failure?
- What anti ice and de icing equipment do you have on your aircraft?
- What anti-icing, de-icing equipment does the B747 have?
- Can you take off with frost on the wings?
- You have been de-iced when does the hold over time begin?
- How does ant-skid work on your aircraft?
- What is TCAS, ETOPS, RVSM, EGPWS?
- What do you know about PRM?
- What is RNP?
- What are the 4 Climb out segments and what are the gradients required for a 2 engine aircraft?
- If you have a tire blow out at V1 what are you actions?
- Why do aircraft have both AC and DC power?
- Define Final Approach fix?
- On this chart it has "no circling" in this area, why and what does it mean?

- What is the Cat C circling area, how is it calculated?
- Describe Circadian Rhythm?
- What is the Validity of the QNH on an ATIS?
- Is the wind direction given on an ATIS true or magnetic?
- What is the ITCZ (Inter Tropical Convergence Zone)?
- What does TSGR mean on a TAF?
- What is the holding speed, timing and direction when below FL140?
- Flying at FL220 in a holding pattern at 300kts, what angle of bank will you use? How long will it take for you to fly one whole pattern?
- When the runway centre lights turn red what does that mean?
- What is the spacing between the runway lights?
- Explain how PAPI works?
- What is a balanced field length?
- What is the definition of V1, V2?
- What factors affect Vmcg, V1, Vmca?
- Why is the windshield heated on larger aircraft?
- Tell us about weather radar?
- Explain how a GPS works?
- What is RAIM?
- What is windshear?
- Windshear warning on ATIS, what are your considerations?
- When can you descend below MDA?
- What is the difference between DA and MDA?
- When can you descend below LSALT at night?
- What is ADS-B what does it depend on?
- What is the climb gradient and obstacle clearance height for a missed approach?
- What engines does your aircraft have?
- Explain how the Turbo Charger works on your aircraft? Where is it located?
- Does your aircraft have a critical engine? Why is it critical?
- What are high bypass engines?
- Do you know what by pass ratio the B777 has?
- What does the Blue line indicate on the ASI?
- What speed is Vmc (Vmca) on your aircraft? What happens if you fly below that?
- Brief to us how you fly a crosswind landing from short final as if we know nothing about flying?
- What is the tropopause and why do we need to know where it is?
- What rate does the temperature decrease with altitude?
- If you are at FL360 and the ISA deviation is ISA minus 10, what is the OAT?
- If you are at FL330 and descending at 1500fpm, how long will it take you to get to sea level?
- If you had a choice, max weight and had a problem, abort at 10 kts after V1, or continue 10 kts prior to V1, what would you do and why?

Notes

9. SCENARIO BASED QUESTIONS

Building questions can play an important part in an interview, some airlines like to place the candidate under stress by asking a "no win situation" style of question. They want to see how you handle the stress and whether or not you dig yourself a hole and if so how you handle it?

Q   "Your Captain breaks a rule in flight, what do you do about it?"

A   *"I would bring it to his attention, maybe he didn't realize he made the error."*

Q   "Ok now that you have brought it to his attention, he tells you he is a senior check Captain and to mind your own business, what will you do now?"

A   *"I would say that I was new in this position and that my understanding of the Standard Operating Procedures was ... I would explain that I have a command to look forward to and that I would like to keep a clean slate with work and not have any incidents on record, so whilst we fly together do you mind if WE stick to the normal procedures."*

Q   "How far would you take the matter?"

A   *"If it become a flight safety risk such as an unstable approach and no corrective action was taken I would firmly call "Go Around", if there was still no action taken I would be obliged to take over".*

"If it was a blatant act of breaking rules and he continued to do it on the following sectors I would advise him that if he didn't stop that I would be forced to submit a flight safety report"

The best way around awkward situations is to point out the basic facts and the company procedures and then put the onus back on the Captain.

Always give someone the opportunity to own up to an incident before you go and report it to the chief pilot, always inform the person you are going to report him or her.

Q   "You smell alcohol on the Captains breath, what are you going to do about it?"

A   *"I would take the Captain aside. I would explain that I can smell alcohol on his breath and that I was concerned. I would strongly advise him to report unfit for duty, emphasising that if I can smell the alcohol then someone else will too, a member of our cabin crew, an airport security officer, a passenger. I would also ask him if his career was worth risking or would it actually be better to call in sick explaining how I would easily handle the situation while the standby pilot was called out"."*

Q   "And if he refused or denied it?"

A   *"I would ask him not to put me into a position where I would have to report him"*

Explain the facts, the consequences and offer a solution.

Notes

10. DO YOU HAVE ANY QUESTIONS FOR US?

There are several ways to approach this.

Usually at the end of the interview they will discuss with you the process from here on.

Now if this is the case in your interview then you could easily end by saying;

"I was curious to know if successful what the process would be from now, however you have informed clearly what to expect, thank you"

Or should they not end on that note then you can ask,

"Can you explain the next stage of the interview process please?"

Other good examples are

"Looking at someone from my background where do you see the biggest challenge in joining the company and can you suggest what I can do to prepare myself in order to have the best start?"

"What do you enjoy most about working for Delta Airlines"

I particularly like this question although some find it hard to ask. It almost always guarantees the interview finishes on a positive note as the interviewer will normally smile, sit up and start talking the virtues of the company.

It also shows you are genuine in wanting to be happy within the organization and are looking at a long term career.

If, during the interview you felt you haven't fully sold yourself here is your opportunity.

"No I don't have any questions, however I would just like to say thank you so much for this opportunity today, should I be successful let me just say that you will gain a very dedicated, reliable employee who will fit in well with your company." etc

Don't ask any Questions that can be turned around and used against you.

Q "Where do you see the A350's fitting into the organization?"

A *"Why don't you tell us?"*

Q "I have done some study on the A330 and I was wondering how the flight controls work in Alternate Law?"

A *"Why don't you tell us what you do know about the flight controls of the A330 and we can go from there?"*

Get the idea?, Don't allow yourself to be opened up to further critique.

Notes

11. TOP 50 INTERVIEW QUESTIONS

- Tell us about your career to date?
- Why did you want to be a pilot?
- What do your parents think of your chosen career?
- What motivates you?
- How do you motivate others?
- What goal are you yet to achieve?
- Where do you see yourself in 5 years, 10 years?
- Name a highlight of your career.
- What was the lowest point in your career?
- Have you ever failed any aviation tests? Flight test, written test? What did you do to pass it in the end?
- What is a weakness of yours?
- How would your best friend describe you?
- How would your Chief Pilot describe you?
- Does your Chief Pilot know you are here today? Do they support you being here?
- What don't you like about your current position?
- How would you change the company you work for now?
- When have you worked with someone different from you?
- What do you admire most about your immediate superiors and why?
- Who do you admire most in your family, why?
- What was your toughest subject at school/university/aviation? Why?
- What was your favourite subject, why?
- Any accidents or incidents, tell us about them?
- Tell me about a difficult decision you had to make in the last year?
- When have you been flexible and worked around a standard operating procedure in order to get the job done.
- What attributes do you believe a good airline captain possess?
- Why do you want to work for us?
- How do you see yourself helping our organisation?
- How important do you think on time performance is for our company?
- Who is the CEO, Chairman, Chief Pilot of our company?
- How many aircraft do we have, types, how many on order, types?
- What is our share price?
- What was our profit last year?
- Do you know what bases we have on offer to our pilot's?
- Tell me about a time you had conflict at work?
- Are you willing to live anywhere?
- What are our destinations?
- Do you know anyone who works here?
- What would you say has been a challenge for our company in the last year?
- What do you think will be a challenge for our company in the near future?
- In our companies history what do you consider is the lowest point? The highest point?
- What is the role of a First Officer?
- Do you know how long you can expect be in our company before you can upgrade to Captain?
- When have you had to think quickly & on the spot?

- Do you think you will be happy living in this country?
- What will you do during your time off?
- Why don't you want to live in your own country?
- What do you see is the biggest personal challenge about joining our company?
- Tell me about a moment when you would have preferred to have been on the ground?
- What will you do if you don't get this position?
- Do you have any questions for us?

NOTES

_____

_____

_____

_____

_____

_____

_____

_____

_____

_____

_____

_____

_____

_____

_____

_____

_____

_____

_____

_____

_____

_____

_____

_____

_____

NOTES

12. GROUP EXERCISES

During the group exercises you will be separated into groups of 8-10 and assigned identical tasks to the other groups. There is normally a time limit and some form of a problem to solve. Sometimes you will be given a problem to solve without all of the information and other times it may require using your own experience and knowledge to complete a task. Use whatever facilities or equipment you have available to you in the classroom. A whiteboard/ chairs/ tables/ clock etc. Try to be as collaborative, organised and professional as possible."

You will be observed from a distance by the facilitators. They will observe how you behave in a team environment.

The facilitators are looking for a variety of characteristics. These can be summarized below.

- Team interaction and participation.
- Ability to speak up and voice your own opinion in front of the group.
- Leadership skills without being overbearing.
- Ability to follow orders.
- Friendliness and respect towards your work colleagues.
- Your overall personality.

The facilitators on the day are looking for an overall behavior that will suit their airlines own aircrew profile. Always be upbeat and positive. Don't be afraid to speak up if required, however remember to follow instructions and respect others in the group. Balance is the key.

If for some reason you find yourself in the position of having to lead the group, there are some simple tips you can use so to avoid getting the wrong type of attention

Sit down and rejoin the group as much as possible, but from a leadership point of view. Avoid lingering around a white board longer than you have to, and once again, wherever possible sit back down and rejoin the group.

By doing this your displaying to the observers your ability to lead the team from within, discussing issues in a group environment rather than simply standing up and writing on a white board.

It also has the effect of moving the attention from yourself back to the group. Offer up the discussion to all in the group exercise and share responsibilities.

Your ability to delegate will be noticed and is a great trait to show in this instance.

Beware of making assumptions i.e. in group exercises sometimes you are given a list of potential job seekers CV's to chose from. Don't assume the gender of someone purely based on their name, many names can be used for either male or female.

 **Tips!**

- Remember your manners
- Pay attention, follow the directions and get involved.
- DO build on something someone else has said.
- Do include others in the conversation, be collaborative.
- DO make your points and if criticised, be prepared to stand up for yourself and diplomatically point out why you believe your opinions are valid.
- DO NOT interrupt someone when they are expressing their ideas.
- DO NOT reject someone else's idea without a good reason.
- DO NOT be overbearing.
- DO NOT sit quietly while other candidates make their points without making your own.
- DO help the group reach a conclusion in the time allocated.

EXAMPLES

1. Complete a jigsaw puzzle where other groups may have some of your pieces. Thereby looking at group to group interaction.
2. Emergency situation problem solving, like being stranded in the south pole, what equipment would you take to walk to base camp, choose only 20 items from the 40 items available?
3. Stranded in the desert, what equipment would you like to have if you could have 10 items, list them in order or importance.
4. Job candidates and a position sought. Work out the best candidate for the position. Different information given on different cards and you are not informed of these differences.

Group Exercise Detailed Example 1

On your way back from a holiday in South America, your shuttle flight to the airport is forced to make an emergency landing in a small clearing in the Brazilian rainforest. You, the pilot, and your fellow passengers have only sustained minor injuries but the plane has broken into pieces and the communication equipment has been destroyed in the impact.

Before the plane crashed the pilot had reported a problem with one of the engines, so there is a good chance that the authorities will start looking for you when you fail to arrive at your destination. However, the forest is very dense and it will take days to reach the edge of it on foot.

You cannot remain where you are as there is a danger that the aeroplane fuel will catch fire. On searching through the wreckage and the remains of your suitcases you find the following items:

A guide to South American plant species

3 elasticated luggage straps

6 frozen airline meals

4 blankets from the plane

A pack of 24 anti-malaria tablets

A 3 metre square piece of opaque plastic sheeting

Tourist map of Brazil

2 large bottles of factor 12 sunscreen

Mobile phone with GPS, fully charged

1 litre bottle of the local alcoholic spirit

3 boxes of chocolate chip cookies

4 current paperback novels

First aid box

Compass Flare gun with one flare

A Swiss Army knife

A book of matches from the hotel

You are unable to carry more than 7 items from this list. (items containing more than one object still count as one item). This is an example of one kind of group exercise that you may encounter at an assessment centre:

- You and your group have found yourselves in a perilous situation as described in the above document. There is a long list of items that you can use to aid your survival, but you can only take a small number of these items with you (the number will be specified).

- Your task is to work out between yourselves which items you will take, and explain why you have chosen these items.

- The assessors will normally watch from the edge of the room, with each assessor focusing on a specific candidate. They will play no part in the exercise and you will normally forget they are there.

- There will be no definite right or wrong answer to this task; the assessors are interested more in how you work as a team and the process through which you come to a group consensus. Group members will be scored on their individual input, rather than the overall result for the group, so someone may still do very well in a team that has failed to reach a conclusion.

- The exercise will usually last 15 to 20 minutes. At the end of the exercise, a member of the group will be asked to write a list of chosen items on a flip chart.

Read through the attached exercise, and if possible, try it out with some friends.

Group Exercise Detailed Example 2 with answers

Included is information from the facilitators point of view and handy tips.

You and your companions have just survived the crash of a small plane. Both the pilot and copilot were killed in the crash. It is mid-January, and you are in Northern Canada. The daily temperature is 25 below zero, and the nighttime temperature is 40 below zero. There is snow on the ground, and the countryside is wooded with several creeks crisscrossing the area. The nearest town is 20 miles away. You are all dressed in city clothes appropriate for a business meeting. Your group of survivors managed to salvage the following items:

A ball of steel wool

A small ax

A loaded .45-caliber pistol

Can of Crisco shortening

Newspapers (one per person)

Cigarette lighter (without fluid)

Extra shirt and pants for each survivor

20 x 20 ft. piece of heavy-duty canvas

A sectional air map made of plastic

One quart of 100-proof whiskey

A compass

Family-size chocolate bars (one per person)

Your task as a group is to list the above 12 items in order of importance for your survival. List the uses for each. You MUST come to agreement as a group.

Your task as a group is to list the above 12 items in order of importance for your survival. List the uses for each. You MUST come to agreement as a group.

EXPLANATION

Mid-January is the coldest time of year in Northern Canada. The first problem the survivors face is the preservation of body heat and the protection against its loss. This problem can be solved by building a fire, minimizing movement and exertion, using as much insulation as possible, and constructing a shelter.

The participants have just crash-landed. Many individuals tend to overlook the enormous shock reaction this has on the human body, and the deaths of the pilot and copilot increases the shock. Decision-making under such circumstances is extremely difficult. Such a situation requires a strong emphasis on the use of reasoning for making decisions and for reducing fear and panic. Shock would be shown in the survivors by feelings of helplessness, loneliness, hopelessness, and fear. These feelings have brought about more fatalities than perhaps any other cause in survival situations. Certainly the state of shock means the movement of the survivors should be at a minimum, and that an attempt to calm them should be made.

Before taking off, a pilot has to file a flight plan which contains vital information such as the course, speed, estimated time of arrival, type of aircraft, and number of passengers. Search-and-rescue operations begin shortly after the failure of a plane to appear at its destination at the estimated time of arrival.

The 20 miles to the nearest town is a long walk under even ideal conditions, particularly if one is not used to walking such distances. In this situation, the walk is even more difficult due to shock, snow, dress, and water barriers. It would mean almost certain death from freezing and exhaustion. At temperatures of minus 25 to minus 40, the loss of body heat through exertion is a very serious matter.

Once the survivors have found ways to keep warm, their next task is to attract the attention of search planes. Thus, all the items the group has salvaged must be assessed for their value in signaling the group's whereabouts.

The ranking of the survivors items was made by Mark Wanvig, a former instructor in survival training for the Reconnaissance School of the 101st Division of the U.S. Army. Mr. Wanvig currently conducts wilderness survival training programs in the Minneapolis, Minnesota area. This survival simulation game is used in military training classrooms.

RANKINGS

1. Cigarette lighter (without fluid)

The gravest danger facing the group is exposure to cold. The greatest need is for a source of warmth and the second greatest need is for signaling devices. This makes building a fire the first order of business. Without matches, something is needed to produce sparks, and even without fluid, a cigarette lighter can do that.

2. Ball of steel wool

To make a fire, the survivors need a means of catching he sparks made by the cigarette lighter. This is the best substance for catching a spark and supporting a flame, even if the steel wool is a little wet.

3. Extra shirt and pants for each survivor

Besides adding warmth to the body, clothes can also be used for shelter, signaling, bedding, bandages, string (when unraveled), and fuel for the fire.

4. Can of Crisco shortening

This has many uses. A mirror-like signaling device can be made from the lid. After shining the lid with steel wool, it will reflect sunlight and generate 5 to 7 million candlepower. This is bright enough to be seen beyond the horizon. While this could be limited somewhat by the trees, a member of the group could climb a tree and use the mirrored lid to signal search planes. If they had no other means of signaling than this, they would have a better than 80% chance of being rescued within the first day.

There are other uses for this item. It can be rubbed on exposed skin for protection against the cold. When melted into an oil, the shortening is helpful as fuel. When soaked into a piece of cloth, melted shortening will act like a candle. The empty can is useful in melting snow for drinking water. It is much safer to drink warmed water than to eat snow, since warm water will help retain body heat. Water is important because dehydration will affect decision-making. The can is also useful as a cup.

5. 20 x 20 foot piece of canvas

The cold makes shelter necessary, and canvas would protect against wind and snow (canvas is used in making tents).

Spread on a frame made of trees, it could be used as a tent or a wind screen. It might also be used as a ground cover to keep the survivors dry. It's shape, when contrasted with the surrounding terrain, makes it a signaling device.

6. Small ax

Survivors need a constant supply of wood in order to maintain the fire. The ax could be used for this as well as for clearing a sheltered campsite, cutting tree branches for ground insulation, and constructing a frame for the canvas tent.

7. Family size chocolate bars (one per person)

Chocolate will provide some food energy. Since it contains mostly carbohydrates, it supplies the energy without making digestive demands on the body.

8. Newspapers (one per person)

These are useful in starting a fire. They can also be used as insulation under clothing when rolled up and placed around a person's arms and legs. A newspaper can also be used as a verbal signaling device when rolled up in a megaphone-shape. It could also provide reading material for recreation.

9. Loaded .45-caliber pistol

The pistol provides a sound-signaling device. (The international distress signal is 3 shots fired in rapid succession). There have been numerous cases of survivors going undetected because they were too weak to make a loud enough noise to attract attention. The butt of the pistol could be used as a hammer, and the powder from the shells will assist in fire building. By placing a small bit of cloth in a cartridge emptied of its bullet, one can start a fire by firing the gun at dry wood on the ground. The pistol also has some serious disadvantages. Anger, frustration, impatience, irritability, and lapses of rationality may increase as the group awaits rescue. The availability of a lethal weapon is a danger to the group under these conditions. Although a pistol could be used in hunting, it would take an expert marksman to kill an animal with it. Then the animal would have to be transported to the crash site, which could prove difficult to impossible depending on its size.

10. Quart of 100 proof whiskey

The only uses of whiskey are as an aid in fire building and as a fuel for a torch (made by soaking a piece of clothing in the whiskey and attaching it to a tree branch). The empty bottle could be used for storing water. The danger of whiskey is that someone might drink it, thinking it would bring warmth. Alcohol takes on the temperature it is exposed to, and a drink of minus 30 degrees Fahrenheit whiskey would freeze a person's esophagus and stomach. Alcohol also dilates the blood vessels in the skin, resulting in chilled blood belong carried back to the heart, resulting in a rapid loss of body heat. Thus, a drunk person is more likely to get hypothermia than a sober person is.

11. Compass

Because a compass might encourage someone to try to walk to the nearest town, it is a dangerous item. It's only redeeming feature is that it could be used as a reflector of sunlight (due to its glass top).

12. Sectional air map made of plastic

This is also among the least desirable of the items because it will encourage individuals to try to walk to the nearest town. It's only useful feature is as a ground cover to keep someone dry.

How to score

Each team should list its top 5 choices in order prior to seeing the answer sheet. To award points, look at the ranking numbers on this answer sheet. Award points to each team's top choices according to the numbers here. For example, the map would earn 12 points, while the steel wool would earn 2 points. Lowest score wins (and survives).

NOTES

_____

_____

_____

_____

_____

_____

13. RESUME AND COVER LETTERS

1. Addressing the letter.

It should be written like any formal letter.

Alignment left. Your name, address, date, receivers name and address.

If you are more comfortable putting your name and address Right alignment then this is still acceptable.

2. To whom it may concern.

Always address the letter to a person, if you don't know the name, call the company/airline and fine out, it must not be address to whom it may concern, this will only speak laziness to your future employer.

3. The opening sentence.

If the position was advertised then write a response to the advertisement. If not then write your expression of interest to a certain position in the company.

"I am writing in response to the Pilot position advertised in the XXX paper on Friday 23rd May."

"I am writing as an expression of interest for a First Officer/Line Pilot position with your company/XXX Airlines."

"I am writing in support of my online application with XXX airlines with the hope of obtaining an interview with your company."

4. The Second Paragraph.

This is where you tell them about your experiences and a brief rundown of what you have been doing and how it would benefit the company.

If you have been out of the industry and trying to get back in, explain your love and passion for aviation, when you gained your CPL and any kind of experience you did gain. Keep it clear and concise.

"I am currently employed with XXX company/airlines flying the XXX aircraft on freight and charter flights throughout the XXX region. I have found this flying to be both rewarding and challenging and I believe this experience has prepared me to fill the position of XXX with your company with confidence."

" I am currently the Chief Pilot for XX and this position has given me experience in such areas as customer relations, recruitment, check and training and most importantly working well as a team member."

5. Your attributes;

Explain what you have to offer the company and the position you are going for. Here you must do your homework on the company and the position being sought. You must match your strengths to the company and what they represent in the industry.

For example if it is for a VIP role on a private Jet, you would highlight your professionalism, maturity, respect for privacy etc.

Or/ If it was for a remote pilot basing for Single Engine charter and mail runs, you would have to highlight your ability to make command decisions, work independently, responsible, reliable etc.

"I will bring to the position dedication, reliability and a willingness to learn and adapt to the role of XXX.I believe that my maturity and passion ……"

"My diverse aviation career has demanded and developed numerous attributes, including leadership, teamwork and skills in customer relations.

"During my career I have always been well respected by both my colleagues and employers. I have taken pride in my professionalism and have developed and honed good interpersonal communication skills."

"Aside from my flying qualifications I take pride in keeping a professional manner. I pay attention to detail, work well in a team environment and know the importance of safety and customers coming first."

Finish the sentence strongly;

"It is these attributes, which if I am successful would allow me to provide a valuable contribution to the XXX team."

"I would like to assure you that if successful with XXX I would prove to be a very loyal, hard working and steadfast member or your team."

"…..loyal, dedicated career employee."

"I am confident that I can make a significant contribution to your airline/company."

Finally

"I look forward to an interview with you soon."

6. The Closing

It is a formal letter so you must end it with Yours Sincerely or Kind Regards.

Leave a gap for your signature and then your name printed below. Sign in blue if possible.

Print below your name "Resume enclosed."

NOTES

_____

_____

_____

_____

_____

_____

_____

_____

_____

_____

_____

_____

_____

_____

_____

_____

_____

_____

_____

_____

SAMPLE LETTER

John Doe
30/28 Woods St
Darwin
N.T. 0800

07 May 2013

Captain Joe Bloggs
Pilot Recruitment Manager
Faraway Airlines
Level 1, 473 Burke St
Melbourne, VIC 3000

Dear Captain Bloggs,

In support of my online application I have enclosed my resume with the aim of being considered for the position of flight crew with Jetstar Airways.

I am currently employed with Hardy Aviation as a line pilot flying charter and freight throughout the Northern Territory region.

During my career I have always been well respected by both my colleagues and management, I have shown passion, loyalty and take pride in my professionalism. My current position has allowed me to hone and develop good interpersonal communication skills and it is these characteristics, which if successful, I will bring to Jetstar.

Thank you for taking the time to read my letter and consider my application and please don't hesitate to contact me should you require further information.

Yours Sincerely

John Doe

AVIATION CURRICULUM VITAE

Your CV should be one page in length and contain certain critical information.

1. Your Contact details must be up to date and accurate.
2. List all of your licences and ratings with expiry dates, include your passport if you are applying for an airline that operates internationally.
3. Flight time should be accurate and rounded to the nearest 10 hrs not the nearest 100 hrs.
4. Aircraft endorsements, you should highlight the endorsements you have that are applicable to the company you are applying for
5. Employment should include a paragraph explaining what your position was within the company and the experience gained. The last 10 yrs of employment only.
6. References, it is always advisable to advise "On Request" this way you can supply the company with the most up to date and relevant referees.

Ally Gregory

56 Fish Rd

Whale

NSW 2090

Australia

PH +61 450438682

Email allyo.g@gmail.com

LICENCES and RATINGS

Australian CPL	No. 594200
Frozen ATPL	
M.E.C.I.R	Exp June 2012
Class 1 Medical	Exp Aug 2012
Australian Passport	No E7594234
ASIC	Exp June 2013

FLIGHT TIME TOTAL: **264**

PIC	71
DUAL	132
NIGHT	13
IFR In-flight	26

ENDORSEMENTS and CERTIFICATES

BE-76	CSU
PN-68	Tailwheel
C210	C180
SE <5700kg	

Dangerous Goods Certificate

First Aid Certificate

EMPLOYMENT

Feb 2011-Current

Skywards Aviation, Sydney

Baggage Handler, Ground based position

2010–Current

Flight Experience, Sydney

B737 Replica Simulator Pilot, Ground based position

EDUCATION

Bachelor of Commerce, 2008

Australian National University, Canberra

Higher School Certificate, 2005

Sydney Public School

REFERENCES

On Request

14. HELP DESK

Should you require any further help with your interview preparation please do not hesitate to contact us at

info@flightdeckconsulting.com

We also offer one on one coaching sessions. Please contact us for further details.

Best of luck with your airline interview.

From the team at FLIGHTDECK CONSULTING.

NOTES

NOTES

_____
_____
_____
_____
_____
_____
_____
_____
_____
_____
_____
_____
_____
_____
_____
_____
_____
_____
_____
_____
_____
_____
_____
_____
_____
_____
_____
_____

NOTES

Made in the USA
Monee, IL
18 January 2020